Number Theory and Fraction Concepts

Glenview, Illinois
Needham, Massachusetts
Upper Saddle River, New Jersey

Staff Credits

Barbara Albright, Janet Fauser, Brian Kane, Marie Mathis, Sandra Morris, Cindy Noftle, Angie Seltzer, David B. Spangler, Jeff Weidenaar

Additional Credits

Steve Curtis Design, Inc., Barbara Hardt, Anne S. Ryan, Stet Graphics, Inc., Ziebka Editorial Services

ISBN: 0-13-043871-5

1 2 3 4 5 6 7 8 9 10   04 03 02 01 00

Number Theory and Fraction Concepts

Table of Contents

Section A Factors and Multiples

Skill 1 Factors and Divisibility 1
Skill 2 Primes and Composites 3
Skill 3 Prime Factorization 5
Skill 4 Exponents 7
Skill 5 Prime Factorization with Exponents 9
Skill 6 Greatest Common Factor 11
Skill 7 Least Common Multiple 13
Skill 8 PROBLEM SOLVING: Draw a Diagram 15
Test Prep 17
Mixed Review 18

Section B Introduction to Fractions

Skill 9 Writing a Fraction as Part of a Set or Part of a Whole 19
Skill 10 Estimating Fractional Amounts 21
Skill 11 Equivalvent Fractions 23
Skill 12 Simplest Form 25
Skill 13 Writing Fractions with the Least Common Denominator 27
Test Prep 29
Mixed Review 30

Section C Fractions, Mixed Numbers, and Decimals

Skill 14 Improper Fractions and Mixed Numbers 31
Skill 15 Improper Fractions, Quotients, and Mixed Numbers.. 33
Skill 16 Comparing and Ordering Fractions and Mixed Numbers 35
Skill 17 Writing Equivalent Fractions and Decimals 37
Skill 18 Dividing to Change a Fraction to a Decimal 39
Test Prep 41
Mixed Review 42

SKILL 1: Factors and Divisibility

Numbers that are multiplied are called **factors**. In $3 \times 8 = 24$, 3 and 8 are the factors. The product, 24, is divisible by each of its factors. When you divide a whole number by one of its factors, the remainder is 0.

To find the factors of a number, you can use divisibility rules. A divisibility rule is a shortcut for determining when one number is divisible by another.

> **A whole number is divisible by:**
> **2** if the ones digit is 0, 2, 4, 6, or 8.
> **3** if the sum of the digits is divisible by 3.
> **5** if the ones digit is 0 or 5.
> **6** if the number is divisible by both 2 and 3.
> **10** if the ones digit is 0.

Example 1

Find the factors of 24.

List all the ways that you could multiply two numbers to get 24.
$1 \times 24 = 24$ $2 \times 12 = 24$ $3 \times 8 = 24$ $4 \times 6 = 24$
The factors of 24 are: 1, 2, 3, 4, 6, 8, 12, 24.

Example 2

By which of these numbers is 78 divisible: 2, 3, 5, 6, or 10?

The ones digit is 8. So, 78 is divisible by 2.
Since $7 + 8 = 15$, and 15 is divisible by 3, 78 is divisible by 3.
Because 78 is divisible by 2 and 3, it is divisible by 6.
The ones digit is not 0 or 5, so it is not divisible by 5 or by 10.

Guided Practice

Find the missing factors of 36.

1. $1 \times$ _____ $= 36$ **2.** $2 \times$ _____ $= 36$ **3.** $3 \times$ _____ $= 36$

4. $4 \times$ _____ $= 36$ **5.** $6 \times$ _____ $= 36$

6. The factors of 36 are: _____.

Write *yes* or *no* to indicate if 1,260 is divisible by the given number.

7. 2 _____   **8.** 3 _____   **9.** 4 _____   **10.** 5 _____

SKILL 1: Practice

Answer each question.

1. Which of the following are factors of 16: 1, 2, 3, 4, 5, 6, 7, 8? _____

2. Which of the following are factors of 20: 1, 2, 3, 4, 5, 6, 7, 8? _____

3. List all factors of 28. _____

4. List all factors of 48. _____

5. List all factors of 100. _____

Complete the table. Write *yes* or *no*.

	Divisible by:				
	2	3	5	6	10
6. 28					
7. 40					
8. 72					
9. 144					
10. 225					
11. 360					
12. 504					
13. 600					

14. There are 365 days in a non-leap year.
    By which of these numbers is 365 divisible: 2, 3, 5, 6, 10? _____

15. Which is not a factor of 54?

    Skill 1

    A 6   **C** 9
    B 7   **D** 27

16. Which is not divisible by 6?

    Skill 1

    F 42   **H** 123
    G 132   **J** 522

SKILL 2: Primes and Composites

Every whole number greater than 1 is either a **prime number** or a **composite number**. A prime number has exactly two factors: itself and 1. A composite number has more than two factors. The numbers 0 and 1 are neither prime nor composite.

Example 1

Is 48 a prime number or a composite number?

The factors of 48 are 1, 2, 3, 4, 6, 8, 12, 16, 24, and 48.

Since there are more than two factors of 48, it is a composite number.

Example 2

Is 57 prime or composite?

Use divisibility rules to decide whether 57 has factors other than 1 and 57.

Is 57 divisible by 2? No; it does not end in 0, 2, 4, 6, or 8.

Is 57 divisible by 3? Yes; 5 + 7 = 12, and 12 is divisible by 3.

57 is composite.

Guided Practice

Tell whether the given number is prime or composite. The factors that follow the number should help you decide.

1. 25: 1, 5, 25

_____

2. 83: 1, 83

_____

3. 54: 1, 2, 3, 6, 9, 18, 27, 54

_____

4. 68: 1, 2, 4, 17, 34, 68

_____

5. Use divisibility rules to help you determine whether 89 is prime or composite.

    a. Is 89 divisible by 2? _____

    b. Is 89 divisible by 3? _____

    c. Is 89 divisible by 5? _____

    d. Is 89 divisible by 7? _____

    e. Is 89 divisible by 8? _____

    f. Is 89 divisible by 9? _____

    g. Is 89 prime or composite? _____

6. List the prime numbers less than 20. _____

7. List the composite numbers less than 20. _____

SKILL 2: Practice

Tell whether the given number is prime or composite. The factors that follow the number should help you decide.

1. 92: 1, 2, 4, 23, 46, 92   **2.** 121: 1, 11, 121   **3.** 73: 1, 73

_____ _____ _____

4. 129: 1, 3, 43, 129   **5.** 52: 1, 2, 4, 13, 26, 52   **6.** 55: 1, 5, 11, 55

_____ _____ _____

7. 29: 1, 29   **8.** 57: 1, 3, 19, 57   **9.** 63: 1, 3, 7, 9, 21, 63

_____ _____ _____

Tell whether each number is prime or composite.

10. 93 _____ **11.** 145 _____

12. 79 _____ **13.** 280 _____

14. 69 _____ **15.** 59 _____

16. 102 _____ **17.** 43 _____

18. 86 _____ **19.** 123 _____

Solve.

20. The Brentwood Orchestra has 161 members.
Is the number of members prime or composite? _____

21. The local Hiking Trails and Open Spaces organization
has 49 members. If a committee of the organization has
a prime number of members, and that number is a factor
of 49, then how many members are on the committee? _____

22. Which of the following is a
prime number?

Skill 2

   A 91   **C** 49

   B 75   **D** 97

23. Which of the following is not
divisible by 4?

Skill 1

   F 1,264   **H** 1,332

   G 414   **J** 748

SKILL 3: Prime Factorization

If a number is prime, then the only way it can be factored is "1 times itself." If a number is composite, it can be expressed as a product of prime factors. This is called its **prime factorization**.

Example 1

Find the prime factorization of 6.

The prime factorization of 6 is 2 × 3, because 2 and 3 are prime and 2 × 3 = 6.

Example 2

Find the prime factorization of 50.

You can use *factor trees* to find prime factors of 50.
Write 50 as the product of two factors.
Is each factor prime or composite?
Circle each prime factor.
Write each composite factor as
the product of two factors.
Continue until all the numbers are prime.

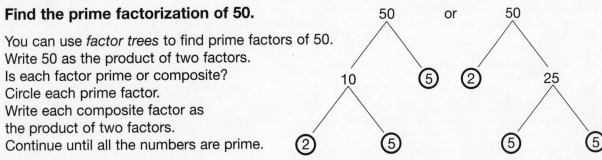

Both factor trees show that 2 × 5 × 5 is the prime factorization of 50.

Guided Practice

Find the prime factorization of each number by writing the appropriate numbers in each blank.

1.

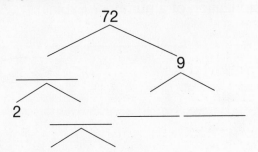

Prime factorization of 72:

_____

2.

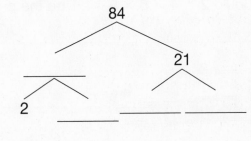

Prime factorization of 84:

_____

3. Is 2 × 6 × 5 the prime factorization of 60? _____

4. Write the prime factorization of 60. _____

5. Is 7 × 12 the prime factorization of 84? _____

SKILL 3: Practice

Find the prime factorization.

1. 12 _____

2. 40 _____

3. 64 _____

4. 36 _____

5. 60 _____

6. 65 _____

7. 20 _____

8. 30 _____

9. 56 _____

10. 21 _____

11. 18 _____

12. 16 _____

13. 630 _____

14. 1,001 _____

15. 625 _____

16. 400 _____

17. 2,000 _____

18. 560 _____

19. The prime factorization of a number is
2 × 2 × 2 × 3 × 3 × 3 × 5 × 5 × 5.
What is the number? _____

20. What number is in the prime factorization of all even numbers? _____

21. Could 2 × 4 × 5 × 9 × 11 be the prime factorization of a number? Explain.

_____

22. Which is the prime factorization
of 48?

Skill 3

A 2 × 2 × 2 × 2 × 3

B 2 × 2 × 2 × 6

C 4 × 12

D 3 × 16

23. Which number is not composite?

Skill 2

F 62

G 77

H 95

J 53

SKILL 4: Exponents

In 5^4, the 4 is the **exponent**. It tells that 5 is to be used as a factor 4 times.

$$\nearrow \mathbf{5^4} \nwarrow$$
base   exponent

5^4 is read "5 to the fourth power."
4^2 is read "4 to the second power."

To compare numbers in exponential form, first find the standard form.
Then compare.

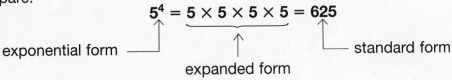

$$5^4 = \underbrace{5 \times 5 \times 5 \times 5} = 625$$

exponential form ⏐   ↑   standard form
expanded form

Example

Compare: $5^3 \bigcirc 3^5$.

We know that $5^3 = 5 \times 5 \times 5$, and $3^5 = 3 \times 3 \times 3 \times 3 \times 3$.

$5 \times 5 \times 5 \bigcirc 3 \times 3 \times 3 \times 3 \times 3$

Write in standard form and compare. $125 < 243$

So, $5^3 < 3^5$.

Guided Practice

1. Write $7 \times 7 \times 7 \times 7 \times 7 \times 7$ in exponential form.

    a. What will the exponent be? ____   **b.** So, $7 \times 7 \times 7 \times 7 \times 7 \times 7 =$ ____.

2. Write 2^5 in standard form.

    a. Write 2^5 in expanded form. _____

    b. Multiply the factors in your answer above. ____

3. Compare: $3^4 \bigcirc 3 + 3 + 3 + 3$. Use $<$, $>$, or $=$.

    a. Write 3^4 in expanded form. _____

    b. Multiply the factors in the expanded form of 3^4. ____

    c. Find the value of $3 + 3 + 3 + 3$. ____

    d. Compare: $3^4 \bigcirc 3 + 3 + 3 + 3$.

SKILL 4: Practice

Write in exponential form.

1. $3 \times 3 \times 3 \times 3 \times 3 \times 3$ _____

2. 53×53 _____

3. $2 \times 2 \times 2 \times 2 \times 2 \times 2 \times 2$ _____

4. $13 \times 13 \times 13$ _____

5. $8 \times 8 \times 8 \times 8$ _____

6. 17×17 _____

Write in expanded form.

7. 10^4 _____

8. 6^5 _____

9. 3^2 _____

10. 7^3 _____

11. 12^4 _____

12. 5^6 _____

Write in standard form.

13. 5^4 _____

14. 2^6 _____

15. 10^7 _____

16. 11^2 _____

17. 12^2 _____

18. 6^3 _____

Compare using <, >, or =.

19. $7^3 \bigcirc 7 + 7 + 7$

20. $3^4 \bigcirc 4^3$

21. $4 \times 10 \bigcirc 10^4$

Solve.

22. The highest point in Kentucky is Black Mountain. Its height is about 2^{12} feet. About how high is Black Mountain?

_____

23. Celeste had 3¢ on Day 1. She had three times that much on Day 2. On Day 3 she had three times as much as she had on Day 2. If she continues this pattern, on what day will she have 2,187¢?

_____

24. Which is 4^3 in standard form?

Skill 4

A 12   **C** 64

B 7   **D** 4

25. Which shows a prime factorization?

Skill 3

F $2 \times 2 \times 3 \times 5$ **H** $3 \times 4 \times 5$

G $2 \times 3 \times 5 \times 6$ **J** 9×12

SKILL 5: Prime Factorization with Exponents

You can use exponents to express prime factorization in a compact form. For example, 125 is equal to $5 \times 5 \times 5$ or 5^3.

To write the prime factorization of 360 in exponential form, first write the factors in expanded form.

$$360 = 2 \times 2 \times 2 \times 3 \times 3 \times 5$$

Use exponents to show the number of identical factors.

two factors of $3 = 3^2$

$$2 \times 2 \times 2 \times 3 \times 3 \times 5 = 2^3 \times 3^2 \times 5$$

three factors of $2 = 2^3$

$5 = 5^1$, but you need not write the exponent.

So, the exponential form of the prime factorization of 360 is $2^3 \times 3^2 \times 5$.

Example

Write the prime factorization $3^3 \times 5^2$ in standard form.

First write in expanded form. $3^3 \times 5^2 = \underbrace{3 \times 3 \times 3}_{27} \times \underbrace{5 \times 5}_{25} = 675$

Then multiply.

The standard form of the number $3^3 \times 5^2$ is 675.

Guided Practice

1. Write $2 \times 2 \times 3 \times 3 \times 3 \times 5 \times 5$ using exponents.

$$2 \times 2 \times 3 \times 3 \times 3 \times 5 \times 5 = 2^{\boxed{}} \times 3^{\boxed{}} \times 5^{\boxed{}}$$

2. Write the prime factorization $2^3 \times 7^2$ in standard form.

a. Write 2^3 in expanded form. _____

b. Multiply the factors in part **a.** _____

c. Write 7^2 in expanded form. _____

d. Multiply the factors in part **c.** _____

e. Multiply the numbers you found in parts **b** and **d.** _____

f. So, $2^3 \times 7^2 = 2 \times$ _____ $\times$ _____ $\times 7 \times$ _____ $= 8 \times$ _____ $=$ _____.

SKILL 5: Practice

Write the prime factorization for each number in expanded form as a product of individual factors. Then write each prime factorization using exponents.

1. 144

_____

_____

2. 90

_____

_____

3. 1,925

_____

_____

4. 480

_____

_____

5. 405

_____

_____

6. 444

_____

_____

7. 128

_____

_____

8. 225

_____

_____

9. 2,600

_____

_____

Write each prime factorization in expanded form. Then write the number in standard form.

10. $2^3 \times 3 \times 5^3$

_____

_____

11. $2^2 \times 3^3 \times 7^2 \times 11$

_____

_____

12. Luis used exponents to write this prime factorization for a number: $2^3 \times 3^3 \times 5^3$
What is the standard form for this number? _____

13. Which is the prime factorization for 720 using exponents?

Skill 5

A $2 \times 2 \times 2 \times 2 \times 3 \times 3 \times 5$

B $2^4 \times 3^2 \times 5$

C $2^3 \times 3^2 \times 5$

D $2 + 2 + 2 + 2 + 3 + 3 + 5$

14. Which is 7^3 in standard form?

Skill 4

F 21

G 37

H 73

J 343

SKILL 6: Greatest Common Factor

Numbers often have common factors. The **greatest common factor** **(GCF)** of two numbers is the greatest number that is a factor of both of them.

Example 1

Find the greatest common factor (GCF) of 24 and 60.

List all factors of 24: **1, 2, 3, 4, 6,** 8, **12**, 24
List all factors of 60: **1, 2, 3, 4,** 5, **6,** 10, **12**, 15, 20, 30, 60

1, 2, 3, 4, 6, and 12 are common factors. The *greatest* common factor is 12.

Example 2

Find the greatest common factor of 24 and 60
by using the prime factorization of each number.

The greatest common factor is the product of the
prime factors that the numbers have in common.

Prime factorization of 24: ②×②× 2 ×③

Prime factorization of 60: ②×②×③× 5

The common prime factors are 2, 2, and 3. So, the greatest
common factor (GCF) is 2 × 2 × 3, or 12.

```
         24                    60
       /    \                /    \
      4      6              4      15
     /\     /\             /\      /\
    2  2   2  3           2  2    3  5
```

Guided Practice

1. Find the GCF of 12 and 18 by listing all factors of each number.

   a. Factors of 12: _____

   b. Factors of 18: _____

   c. GCF: _____

2. Find the GCF of 18 and 90 by using their prime factorizations.

   a. Prime factorization of 18: _____

   b. Prime factorization of 90: _____

   c. The common prime factors of 19 and 90 are: _____, _____, and _____.

   d. The product of the common prime factors is _____.

   e. So, the GCF of 18 and 90 is _____.

SKILL 6: Practice

Find the GCF of each pair of numbers by listing all factors of each number.

1. 28: _____

     35: _____

     GCF: _____

2. 16: _____

     24: _____

     GCF: _____

3. 30: _____

     36: _____

     GCF: _____

4. 24: _____

     42: _____

     GCF: _____

Find the GCF of each pair of numbers by using their prime factorizations.

5. 14: _____

     35: _____

     GCF: _____

6. 18: _____

     27: _____

     GCF: _____

7. 48: _____

     54: _____

     GCF: _____

8. 36: _____

     48: _____

     GCF: _____

9. 40: _____

     80: _____

     GCF: _____

10. 32: _____

     36: _____

     GCF: _____

Solve.

11. Marcel's age is a common factor of both 48 and 72. She is older than 12. How old is Marcel? _____

12. Which is the GCF of 24 and 36?

     Skill 6

     A 3   **C** 2

     B 24   **D** 12

13. Which is the prime factorization of 56 using exponents?

     Skill 5

     F 7×8 **H** $2^2 \times 7$

     G $2^3 \times 7$ **J** 2×28

SKILL 7: Least Common Multiple

The **least common multiple (LCM)** of two or more whole numbers is the smallest number that is a common multiple of the given numbers.

Example 1

Find the least common multiple (LCM) of 6 and 8.

List the first several multiples of each number.

Multiples of 6:   6, 12, 18, ⟨24⟩ 30, 36, 42, ⟨48⟩

Multiples of 8:   8, 16, ⟨24⟩ 32, 40, ⟨48⟩ 56

common multiples

The least common multiple (LCM) of 6 and 8 is 24.

Example 2

Find the least common multiple of 15 and 30.

When one number is a multiple of the other, the larger number is the least common multiple.

30 is 2 × 15, so 30 is a multiple of 15. The least common multiple of 15 and 30 is 30.

Example 3

Find the least common multiple of 30 and 21 by using prime factorization.

Write the prime factors of each number. Circle pairs of common factors as you did to find GCF.

30 = 2 × ⟨3⟩ × 5

21 = ⟨3⟩ × 7

To find the LCM, multiply one number by the uncircled factors of the other number.
The LCM of 30 and 21 = 30 × 7 = 210.

Guided Practice

1. Find the least common multiple of 12 and 16.

   a. List the first six multiples of 12: _____

   b. List the first six multiples of 16: _____

   c. LCM: _____

2. Find the least common multiple of 24 and 48.

   a. Is 48 a multiple of 24? _____   **b.** LCM: _____

3. Find the least common multiple of 6 and 11.

   a. Do 6 and 11 have a common factor? _____   **b.** LCM: _____

SKILL 7: Practice

Find the LCM of each pair of numbers by listing multiples of each number.

1. 3: _____

  2: _____

  LCM: _____

2. 3: _____

  4: _____

  LCM: _____

3. 5: _____

  4: _____

  LCM: _____

4. 2: _____

  8: _____

  LCM: _____

Find the LCM of each pair.

5. 6, 5 _____

6. 3, 21 _____

7. 9, 5 _____

8. 17, 3 _____

9. 6, 23 _____

10. 21, 7 _____

11. 6, 28 _____

12. 14, 18 _____

13. 23, 2 _____

14. 11, 33 _____

15. 6, 10 _____

16. 36, 45 _____

17. 31, 5 _____

18. 10, 14 _____

19. 22, 4 _____

20. 20, 30 _____

21. 29, 3 _____

22. 16, 18 _____

23. 12, 18 _____

24. 20, 25 _____

25. 15, 40 _____

Solve.

26. Hot dogs come 8 to a package. Buns come 6 to a package. What is the fewest number of packages of each you would have to buy so that you have exactly as many hot dogs as buns?

_____ packages of hot dogs; _____ packages of buns

27. Which is the LCM of 15 and 24?

Skill 7

A 3   **C** 9

B 120   **D** 360

28. Which is the GCF of 24 and 40?

Skill 6

F 960   **H** 8

G 120   **J** 4

SKILL 8: PROBLEM SOLVING:
Draw a Diagram

Solving a problem can often be easier if you draw a diagram or picture to help you understand the problem.

Example

Marti has Sunday off, then works Monday through Saturday, so she has a day off once every 7 days. She needs to give her dog some medicine every 3 days. How often does she give her dog medicine on her day off?

Read   Marti's days off occur every 7 days. Her dog needs medicine every 3 days.

Plan   Draw a diagram of several weeks on a calendar. Label her days off with "Off." Label the days her dog needs medicine with "M."

Solve   Start with a Sunday she is off and she gives medicine. Find the next day that this happens.

Sun.	Mon.	Tues.	Wed.	Thurs.	Fri.	Sat.
Off/M			M			M
Off		M			M	
Off	M			M		
Off/M						

Twenty-one days later, Marti has a day off and her dog needs medicine. She gives her dog medicine on her day off every 21 days.

Look Back   Does your answer makes sense? The least common multiple of 7 and 3 is 21. It makes sense that an event occurring every 7 days and another event occurring every 3 days will occur together on the LCM of 7 and 3.

Guided Practice

Ari is buying buns and hamburgers for a picnic. Buns come 8 to a package. Hamburgers come 10 to a package. Ari would like to buy exactly as many hamburgers as buns.

1. Fill in the diagram with the number of items per package to illustrate the fewest number of packages of each item Ari should buy.

Buns   Hamburgers

□ □ □ □ □   □ □ □ □

40 buns   40 hamburgers

2. How many buns and hamburgers will he buy? _____

3. How many packages of each will this be?

____ packages of buns; ____ packages of hamburgers

SKILL 8: Practice

Solve each problem.

1. The bookstore sells packages of 15 pens each and 12 pencils each. They want the same number of pens and pencils in their next order. Find the smallest number of packages of each they can buy.

   _____

2. Ms. Ling's chemistry class uses 10-gram weights and 25-gram weights on a balance scale. What is the smallest number of each needed to balance the scale?

   _____

3. Freida wants to use the same number of black beads and white beads for a project. Black beads come in bags of 20. White beads come in bags of 15. What is the least number of bags of each color she can use?

   _____

4. All Sport Outdoor Store sells fruit energy bars in 6-bar packages. They also sell nut energy bars in 4-bar packages. If the store wants to order the same number of bars of both kinds, what is the least number of packages of each they can order?

   _____

5. The traffic signal at 4th and Main turns green every 6 minutes. The signal at 5th and Broadway turns green every 4 minutes. If both turned green at 12:15 P.M., when are the next three times that both will turn green at the same time?

   _____

6. Boxes that are 10 inches tall are stacked next to boxes that are 12 inches tall. Find the least number of each size box that could be stacked next to each other so that the stacks are the same height.

   Skill 7

   A two 10-in. and two 12-in.

   B twelve 10-in. and ten 12-in.

   C six 10-in. and five 12-in.

   D five 10-in. and six 12-in.

7. Find the GCF of 14 and 24.

   Skill 6

   F 168   **H** 2

   G 3   **J** 38

Name _____   Date _____   Class _____

Circle each correct answer.

1. Which is the standard form for 5^3?

Skill 4

   A 15   **C** 125

   B 53   **D** 35

2. Which is the LCM of 24 and 36?

Skill 7

   F 4   **H** 12

   G 72   **J** 144

3. Which is a prime number?

Skill 2

   A 2   **C** 10

   B 14   **D** 25

4. Which is the GCF of 9 and 12?

Skill 6

   F 108   **H** 21

   G 3   **J** 6

5. Red marbles come in bags of 8. Green marbles come in bags of 6. What is the fewest number of bags of each color you can buy so that you will have the same number of marbles of each color?

Skill 8

   A 2 bags red; 2 bags green

   B 6 bags red; 8 bags green

   C 4 bags red; 3 bags green

   D 3 bags red; 4 bags green

6. 80 is not divisible by which number?

Skill 1

   F 2   **H** 6

   G 10   **J** 5

7. Which is the prime factorization of 144?

Skill 3

   A 12×12

   B $2 \times 2 \times 2 \times 2 \times 3 \times 3$

   C $4 \times 4 \times 9$

   D $2 \times 2 \times 2 \times 3 \times 3 \times 3$

8. Which is divisible by 3?

Skill 1

   F 531   **H** 128

   G 965   **J** 292

9. Which is the LCM of 5 and 7?

Skill 7

   A 7   **C** 1

   B 15   **D** 35

10. Which is the prime factorization of 84?

Skill 5

   F $2 \times 3 \times 7$

   G $2^2 \times 3 \times 7$

   H $2 \times 3^2 \times 7$

   J $2^2 \times 3^2 \times 7$

11. Which has the same value as $3 \times 3 \times 3 \times 3$?

Skill 4

   A 4^3 **C** 4×3

   B 3^4 **D** 27

12. Which is the prime factorization of 675?

Skill 5

   F $3 \times 5 \times 3 \times 5$

   G 25×27

   H $3^3 \times 5^3$

   J $3^3 \times 5^2$

Mixed Review for Section A

State Match-Up

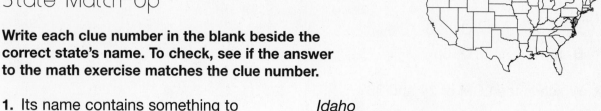

**Write each clue number in the blank beside the
correct state's name. To check, see if the answer
to the math exercise matches the clue number.**

1. Its name contains something to
   write with.

   Idaho
   The standard form for 2^3 _____

2. Its name contains 4 identical vowels.

   Pennsylvania
   The number that is neither
   prime nor composite _____

3. It is surrounded by water.

   Florida
   The LCM of 2 and 3 _____

4. Its name contains the name of
   another state.

   Hawaii
   The prime factorization of 27
   contains this number. _____

5. It has the same name as the capital of
   the United States.

   Mississippi
   32 is this number to the
   fifth power. _____

6. Its southern tip is near Cuba.

   Colorado
   The number that is the prime
   number between 5 and 11 _____

7. It is the home of Pikes Peak in the
   Rocky Mountains.

   Arkansas
   The GCF of 20 and 36 _____

   New York
   This number is the product of
   two factors of 3. _____

8. Its name is the name of a potato.

   Washington
   Rulers come in 4-packs. Erasers come
   in 10-packs. To buy the same number

9. It has a city that has the same name as
   the state.

   of each, buy this number pack of
   rulers and 2 packs of erasers. _____

SKILL 9: Writing a Fraction as Part of a Set or Part of a Whole

Fractions can be used to indicate a part of a set or a part of a whole.

Example 1

In the set of four triangles at the right, three of them are shaded. One of them is not shaded.

a. **What fraction of the set is shaded?**

number of shaded triangles → $\frac{3}{4}$
total number of triangles →

b. **What fraction of the set is not shaded?**

number of triangles not shaded → $\frac{1}{4}$
total number of triangles →

Example 2

The circle at the right is divided into five equal parts. Three of the parts are shaded.

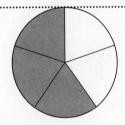

a. **What fraction of the circle is shaded?**

number of shaded parts → $\frac{3}{5}$
total number of parts →

b. **What fraction of the circle is not shaded?**

number of parts not shaded → $\frac{2}{5}$
total number of parts →

Guided Practice

1. What fraction of the cards at the right show odd numbers?

number of odd-numbered cards → ☐
total number of cards → ☐

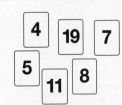

2. What fraction of the figure at the right is shaded?

number of shaded sections → ☐
total number of sections → ☐

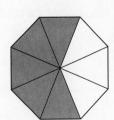

SKILL 9: Practice

Write a fraction to tell what part is shaded.

1.

_____

2.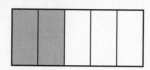

_____

3.

_____

4.

_____

5.

_____

6.

_____

7.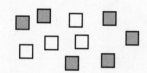

_____

8.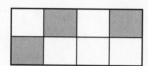

_____

9.

_____

The picture at the right shows how to set up the game of backgammon. The 24 triangular-shaped spaces on the board are called points.

10. What fraction of the points have five black playing pieces?

_____

11. What fraction of the white playing pieces are on the point shown at the upper left corner of the board?

_____

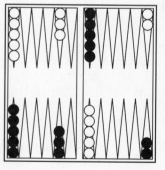

12. Which fractional part is shaded?

Skill 9

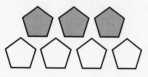

A $\frac{4}{7}$

B $\frac{7}{7}$

C $\frac{3}{7}$

D $\frac{3}{4}$

13. An office supply store sells packages of 6 folders each and 9 labels each. Which is the least number of packages of folders you should buy if you want to buy the same number of folders and labels?

Skill 8

F 2   H 36

G 3   J 18

SKILL 10: Estimating Fractional Amounts

You can estimate fractional amounts by imagining the whole being
divided into equal parts.

Example 1

About how much of the circle at the right is shaded?

Imagine a line through the middle of the circle
dividing it in half as shown.

Since the amount shaded is slightly more than $\frac{1}{2}$ of

the circle, you can estimate that about $\frac{1}{2}$ of the circle is shaded.

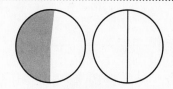

Example 2

About how much of the figure at the right is shaded?

Imagine lines dividing the rectangle into thirds.

Since the amount shaded is slightly less than

$\frac{1}{3}$ of the rectangle, you can estimate that about

$\frac{1}{3}$ of the rectangle is shaded.

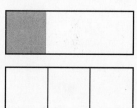

Guided Practice

1. About how much of the rectangle
at the right is shaded?

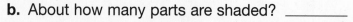

   a. The lines divide the rectangle
      into how many equal parts? _____

   b. About how many parts are shaded? _____

   c. How much of the rectangle would you estimate is shaded? _____

2. About how much of the circle at the right is shaded?

   a. The lines divide the circle

      into how many equal parts? _____

   b. About how many parts are shaded? _____

   c. How much of the circle would you estimate is shaded? _____

SKILL 10: Practice

About how much is shaded?

1.

_____

2.

_____

3.

_____

4.

_____

5.

_____

6.

_____

7.

_____

8.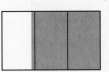

_____

9.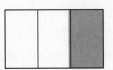

_____

10. The picture at the right shows Anita painting her playhouse. About how much of the front of the playhouse is painted?

_____

TEST PREP

11. Which tells about how much is shaded?

Skill 10

A $\frac{1}{3}$ **C** $\frac{3}{3}$

B $\frac{4}{3}$ **D** $\frac{2}{3}$

12. Which fractional part is shaded?

Skill 9

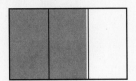

F $\frac{7}{7}$ **H** $\frac{2}{7}$

G $\frac{2}{5}$ **J** $\frac{5}{7}$

SKILL 11: Equivalent Fractions

If two fractions represent the same quantity, they are **equivalent**.

Example 1

Use a model to show that $\frac{1}{2}$ and $\frac{4}{8}$ are equivalent fractions.

Draw a circle divided into two parts and shade $\frac{1}{2}$.

Draw more lines to divide each half into 4 parts. This shows $\frac{4}{8}$.

$\frac{1}{2} = \frac{4}{8}$

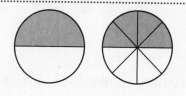

Example 2

Find two fractions that are equivalent to $\frac{5}{10}$.

Multiply or divide the numerator and the denominator by the same nonzero number. This is the same as multiplying or dividing the fraction by 1.

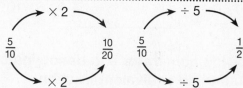

numerator $\longrightarrow$
denominator $\longrightarrow$ $\frac{5 \times 2}{10 \times 2} = \frac{10}{20}$ So, $\frac{5}{10}$ is equivalent to $\frac{10}{20}$.

numerator $\longrightarrow$
denominator $\longrightarrow$ $\frac{5 \div 5}{10 \div 5} = \frac{1}{2}$ So, $\frac{5}{10}$ is equivalent to $\frac{1}{2}$.

Guided Practice

1. Find a fraction equivalent to $\frac{2}{3}$.
   Use the models at the right.

   $\frac{2}{3} = $ _____

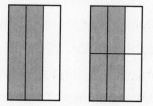

2. Multiply to find an equivalent fraction.

   $\frac{2}{6} = \frac{2 \times \boxed{}}{6 \times \boxed{}} = \frac{\boxed{}}{\boxed{}}$

3. Divide to find an equivalent fraction.

   $\frac{6}{8} = \frac{6 \div \boxed{}}{8 \div \boxed{}} = \frac{\boxed{}}{\boxed{}}$

Name _____ Date _____ Class _____

SKILL 11: Practice

Use the models to find an equivalent fraction.

1.

$\frac{2}{5} =$ _____

2.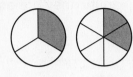

$\frac{1}{3} =$ _____

3.

$\frac{1}{2} =$ _____

Multiply numerator and denominator by the given number to find an equivalent fraction.

4. $3; \frac{4}{7} =$ _____

5. $2; \frac{1}{6} =$ _____

6. $5; \frac{2}{3} =$ _____

7. $6; \frac{5}{8} =$ _____

8. $10; \frac{2}{11} =$ _____

9. $8; \frac{3}{5} =$ _____

Divide numerator and denominator by the given number to find an equivalent fraction.

10. $2; \frac{10}{12} =$ _____

11. $6; \frac{36}{42} =$ _____

12. $5; \frac{20}{30} =$ _____

13. $9; \frac{27}{45} =$ _____

14. $10; \frac{50}{80} =$ _____

15. $4; \frac{44}{64} =$ _____

16. Find an equivalent fraction for $\frac{10}{18}$ that has a smaller denominator.

17. Find an equivalent fraction for $\frac{9}{14}$ that has a larger denominator.

18. Find an equivalent fraction for $\frac{30}{36}$ that has a smaller denominator. Then find one with a larger denominator.

 TEST PREP

19. Which is equivalent to $\frac{4}{5}$?   *Skill 11*

A $\frac{6}{7}$ C $\frac{4}{10}$

B $\frac{12}{15}$ D $\frac{2}{10}$

20. Which tells about how full the glass is?   *Skill 10*

F $\frac{1}{4}$ H $\frac{3}{4}$

G $\frac{1}{2}$ J $\frac{1}{8}$

Name	Date	Class

SKILL 12: Simplest Form

A fraction is in simplest form when the only common factor of the numerator and the denominator is 1.

Example 1

Write $\frac{8}{24}$ in simplest form.

Divide the numerator and the denominator by a common factor.	$\rightarrow$	Continue dividing if there are still common factors (other than 1).	$\rightarrow$	The fraction is in simplest form because the only common factor of 1 and 3 is 1.

$$\frac{8 \div 2}{24 \div 2} = \frac{4}{12}$$

not in simplest form

$$\frac{4 \div 4}{12 \div 4} = \frac{1}{3}$$

in simplest form

$$\frac{8}{24} = \frac{1}{3}$$

Example 2

Write $\frac{36}{42}$ in simplest form.

To write a fraction in simplest form, you can divide the numerator and the denominator by their greatest common factor (GCF).

Factors of 36: **1**, **2**, **3**, 4, **6**, 9, 12, 18, 36

Factors of 42: **1**, **2**, **3**, **6**, 7, 14, 21, 42

The GCF is 6.

$$\frac{36}{42} = \frac{36 \div 6}{42 \div 6} = \frac{6}{7}$$

$\frac{6}{7}$ is in simplest form.

Guided Practice

1. Write $\frac{4}{10}$ in simplest form.

   a. What is the GCF of 4 and 10? _____

   b. Divide numerator and denominator by your answer to part **a.**

$$\frac{4 \div \square}{10 \div \square} = \frac{\square}{\square}$$

2. Write $\frac{32}{40}$ in simplest form. _____

SKILL 12: Practice

Find the GCF of the numerator and denominator in each fraction. Then write the fraction in simplest form.

1. $\frac{6}{9}$

   GCF: _____

   Simplest form: _____

2. $\frac{10}{40}$

   GCF: _____

   Simplest form: _____

3. $\frac{28}{48}$

   GCF: _____

   Simplest form: _____

Write in simplest form.

4. $\frac{12}{24}$ _____

5. $\frac{9}{21}$ _____

6. $\frac{8}{10}$ _____

7. $\frac{6}{28}$ _____

8. $\frac{18}{20}$ _____

9. $\frac{30}{38}$ _____

10. $\frac{8}{20}$ _____

11. $\frac{12}{18}$ _____

12. $\frac{14}{32}$ _____

13. $\frac{8}{12}$ _____

14. $\frac{12}{16}$ _____

15. $\frac{12}{30}$ _____

16. $\frac{9}{15}$ _____

17. $\frac{6}{42}$ _____

18. $\frac{9}{12}$ _____

19. $\frac{6}{15}$ _____

20. $\frac{6}{10}$ _____

21. $\frac{6}{12}$ _____

22. $\frac{24}{30}$ _____

23. $\frac{21}{28}$ _____

24. $\frac{14}{24}$ _____

25. $\frac{36}{48}$ _____

26. $\frac{16}{52}$ _____

27. $\frac{18}{81}$ _____

28. A kilometer is about $\frac{6}{10}$ of a mile.

    Write this fraction in simplest form.   _____

29. Last week, $\frac{25}{30}$ of the students in Mr. Lim's class went on a field trip. Write this fraction in simplest form.   _____

30. The band members make up $\frac{35}{100}$ students at Winfield Middle School. Write this fraction in simplest form.   _____

31. Which is in simplest form?   *Skill 12*

    A $\frac{9}{16}$ C $\frac{9}{18}$

    B $\frac{6}{15}$ D $\frac{8}{14}$

32. Which is equivalent to $\frac{5}{8}$?   *Skill 11*

    F $\frac{6}{10}$ H $\frac{3}{4}$

    G $\frac{10}{14}$ J $\frac{20}{32}$

SKILL 13: Writing Fractions with the Least Common Denominator

The **least common denominator (LCD)** of two or more fractions is the number that is the LCM of their denominators.

Once you have found the least common denominator, write equivalent fractions with this denominator.

Example

Find the least common denominator for $\frac{5}{8}$ and $\frac{1}{12}$. Then write an equivalent fraction for each, using the least common denominator.

The denominators are 8 and 12.

Multiples of 8: 8, 16, **24**, 32, 40

Multiples of 12: 12, **24**, 36, 48

The LCM of 8 and 12 is 24.

Write an equivalent fraction of $\frac{5}{8}$ and $\frac{1}{12}$, using 24 as the denominator.

Since $8 \times 3 = 24$, multiply 5 by 3 to obtain the numerator.

$$\frac{5}{8} = \frac{5 \times 3}{8 \times 3} = \frac{15}{24}$$

Since $12 \times 2 = 24$, multiply 1 by 2 to obtain the numerator.

$$\frac{1}{12} = \frac{1 \times 2}{12 \times 2} = \frac{2}{24}$$

So, using the LCD of 24, $\frac{5}{8} = \frac{15}{24}$ and $\frac{1}{2} = \frac{2}{24}$.

Guided Practice

1. Write $\frac{1}{3}$ and $\frac{3}{4}$ as equivalent fractions with the least common denominator.

   a. What is the LCM for 3 and 4? _____

   b. By what number will you multiply
      the numerator and denominator of $\frac{1}{3}$? _____

   c. $\dfrac{1 \times \square}{3 \times \square} = \dfrac{\square}{\square}$

   d. By what number will you multiply
      the numerator and denominator of $\frac{3}{4}$? _____

   e. $\dfrac{3 \times \square}{4 \times \square} = \dfrac{\square}{\square}$

2. Write $\frac{1}{2}$ and $\frac{1}{3}$ as equivalent fractions
with the least common denominator.

_____

SKILL 13: Practice

Find the LCM for each pair of numbers.

1. 4, 5 _____   **2.** 6, 9 _____   **3.** 8, 10 _____   **4.** 6, 8 _____

5. 9, 12 _____   **6.** 4, 8 _____   **7.** 6, 7 _____   **8.** 5, 10 _____

Find the least common denominator for each pair of fractions. Then write an equivalent fraction for each, using the least common denominator.

9. $\frac{3}{5}, \frac{1}{2}$

LCD: _____

10. $\frac{1}{6}, \frac{4}{7}$

LCD: _____

11. $\frac{3}{4}, \frac{3}{8}$

LCD: _____

_____   _____   _____

Write an equivalent fraction for each, using the least common denominator.

12. $\frac{7}{9}, \frac{1}{6}$

13. $\frac{1}{2}, \frac{9}{10}$

14. $\frac{5}{8}, \frac{3}{7}$

_____   _____   _____

15. $\frac{5}{9}, \frac{3}{10}$

16. $\frac{4}{7}, \frac{1}{2}$

17. $\frac{3}{8}, \frac{3}{5}$

_____   _____   _____

18. $\frac{5}{12}, \frac{5}{6}$

19. $\frac{1}{4}, \frac{7}{8}$

20. $\frac{2}{5}, \frac{2}{7}$

_____   _____   _____

21. $\frac{11}{15}, \frac{3}{5}$

22. $\frac{5}{12}, \frac{7}{16}$

23. $\frac{13}{18}, \frac{17}{24}$

_____   _____   _____

24. Keri keeps her computer CDs on two shelves. One shelf is $\frac{3}{4}$ full. The other is $\frac{5}{6}$ full. Write an equivalent fraction for each, using the least common denominator. _____

25. What is the least common denominator for $\frac{5}{6}$ and $\frac{3}{8}$?

Skill 13

A 48   **C** 12

B 24   **D** 16

26. Which is the simplest form?

Skill 12

F $\frac{10}{12}$ **H** $\frac{9}{14}$

G $\frac{4}{6}$ **J** $\frac{7}{21}$

TEST PREP FOR SECTION B

Circle each correct answer.

1. Which is equivalent to $\frac{3}{8}$?

Skill 11

A $\frac{6}{8}$ **C** $\frac{3}{4}$

B $\frac{9}{24}$ **D** $\frac{3}{16}$

2. Which shows the shaded part?

Skill 9

F $\frac{1}{4}$ **H** $\frac{4}{4}$

G $\frac{1}{3}$ **J** $\frac{3}{4}$

3. Which is in simplest form?

Skill 12

A $\frac{4}{9}$ **C** $\frac{4}{6}$

B $\frac{3}{6}$ **D** $\frac{10}{12}$

4. Which tells about how much is shaded?

Skill 10

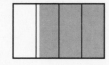

F $\frac{2}{3}$ **H** $\frac{1}{2}$

G $\frac{3}{4}$ **J** $\frac{9}{10}$

5. What is the least common denominator for $\frac{2}{5}$ and $\frac{1}{3}$?

Skill 13

A 3   **C** 15

B 5   **D** 30

6. Which is in simplest form?

Skill 12

F $\frac{4}{6}$ **H** $\frac{6}{9}$

G $\frac{4}{12}$ **J** $\frac{2}{3}$

7. Which shows the shaded part?

Skill 9

A $\frac{5}{6}$ **C** $\frac{1}{5}$

B $\frac{1}{5}$ **D** $\frac{5}{1}$

8. Which is equivalent to $\frac{30}{36}$?

Skill 11

F $\frac{18}{15}$ **H** $\frac{10}{12}$

G $\frac{4}{6}$ **J** $\frac{24}{30}$

9. Which tells about how full the jar is?

Skill 10

A $\frac{2}{3}$ **C** $\frac{1}{2}$

B $\frac{3}{4}$ **D** $\frac{1}{3}$

10. Which shows an equivalent fraction for $\frac{5}{8}$ and an equivalent fraction for $\frac{5}{6}$, using the LCD?

Skill 13

F $\frac{15}{24}$; $\frac{20}{24}$ **H** $\frac{5}{24}$; $\frac{20}{24}$

G $\frac{30}{48}$; $\frac{40}{48}$ **J** $\frac{10}{24}$; $\frac{20}{24}$

11. Which is equivalent to $\frac{24}{28}$?

Skill 11

A $\frac{20}{24}$ **C** $\frac{30}{34}$

B $\frac{12}{14}$ **D** $\frac{12}{16}$

12. Which shows an equivalent fraction for $\frac{7}{9}$ and an equivalent fraction for $\frac{5}{6}$, using the LCD?

Skill 13

F $\frac{7}{12}$; $\frac{10}{12}$ **H** $\frac{42}{54}$; $\frac{45}{54}$

G $\frac{14}{18}$; $\frac{15}{18}$ **J** $\frac{7}{18}$; $\frac{5}{18}$

Name _____ Date _____ Class _____

 Mixed Review for Section B

Why can't a bicycle stand by itself?

To find out why, find the answer to each exercise at the bottom of the page and write the letter on the blank above the answer.

U **1.** Tell how much is shaded. _____

E **2.** $\frac{3}{5}$ is equivalent $\frac{\square}{10}$. _____

W **3.** What part is shaded? _____

I **4.** What is simplest form for $\frac{14}{24}$? _____

T **5.** Tell about how full the jar is. _____

T **6.** What is the least common denominator of $\frac{5}{6}$ and $\frac{1}{4}$? _____

T **7.** What is simplest form for $\frac{15}{36}$? _____

I **8.** $\frac{24}{32}$ is equivalent to $\frac{6}{\square}$. _____

R **9.** $\frac{8}{26}$ is equivalent $\frac{\square}{78}$. _____

E **10.** What is simplest form for $\frac{20}{28}$? _____

O **11.** What part is shaded?  _____

S **12.** What is simplest form for $\frac{42}{48}$? _____

C **13.** Rewrite $\frac{1}{3}$ and $\frac{5}{12}$ using the LCD. _____

E **14.** Rewrite $\frac{7}{12}$ and $\frac{9}{16}$ using the LCD. _____

S **15.** $\frac{28}{35}$ is equivalent to $\frac{4}{\square}$. _____

D **16.** What is simplest form for $\frac{48}{56}$? _____

A **17.** What is the least common denominator of $\frac{1}{12}$ and $\frac{3}{14}$? _____

B **18.** What part is shaded?  _____

$\frac{5}{6}$ 6 $\frac{4}{12};\frac{5}{12}$ 84 $\frac{3}{4}$ $\frac{7}{8}$ $\frac{5}{7}$ $\frac{7}{12}$ $\frac{5}{12}$ 5

12 $\frac{3}{8}$ $\frac{1}{4}$ $\frac{1}{2}$ 8 24 $\frac{28}{48},\frac{27}{48}$ $\frac{6}{7}$

SKILL 14: Improper Fractions and Mixed Numbers

An improper fraction has a numerator that is greater than or equal to its denominator. So, it has a value greater than or equal to 1. A mixed number shows the sum of a whole number and a fraction.

Example 1

Write an improper fraction and a mixed number to describe the picture at the right.

The shapes are divided into fifths, so the denominator of the fraction will be 5. There are 12 shaded parts, so the numerator will be 12.

$\dfrac{12}{5}$ ← 12 shaded parts
← all parts are fifths

There are 2 wholes shaded.
The third shape has 2 fifths shaded.

two wholes → $2\dfrac{2}{5}$ ← 2 shaded parts
← all parts are fifths

The improper fraction $\dfrac{12}{5}$ and the mixed number $2\dfrac{2}{5}$ are equivalent.

Example 2

Write $3\dfrac{1}{4}$ as an improper fraction.

Step 1: Multiply the denominator by the whole number.

Step 2: Add the numerator.

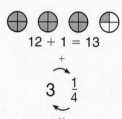

$12 + 1 = 13$

Step 3: Use the sum from Step 2 as the numerator of the improper fraction. Use the denominator of the fraction.

$3 \quad \dfrac{1}{4}$

So, $3\dfrac{1}{4} = \dfrac{13}{4}$. The improper fraction is $\dfrac{13}{4}$.

$4 \times 3 = 12$

Guided Practice

1. Write an improper fraction and a mixed number to describe the picture at the right. _____

2. Write $3\dfrac{4}{5}$ as an improper fraction.

   a. How many fifths are in 3 wholes? _____

   b. How many total fifths? _____

   c. Improper fraction: _____

Name _____ Date _____ Class _____

SKILL 14: Practice

Write an improper fraction and a mixed number to describe
each picture.

1.

_____

2.

_____

3.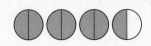

_____

4.

_____

5.

_____

6.

_____

Write each mixed number as an improper fraction.

7. $2\frac{1}{6}$ _____

8. $5\frac{1}{5}$ _____

9. $1\frac{2}{5}$ _____

10. $13\frac{1}{2}$ _____

11. $8\frac{3}{4}$ _____

12. $3\frac{2}{3}$ _____

13. $14\frac{2}{9}$ _____

14. $12\frac{2}{3}$ _____

15. $3\frac{5}{8}$ _____

16. $9\frac{1}{9}$ _____

17. $7\frac{4}{5}$ _____

18. $8\frac{1}{3}$ _____

19. $4\frac{1}{4}$ _____

20. $9\frac{1}{2}$ _____

21. $12\frac{1}{3}$ _____

22. $2\frac{4}{7}$ _____

Solve.

23. Muriel counted 17 quarters in her bank. Write the amount
of money she has in her bank as a mixed number. _____

24. Which shows the improper
fraction for $6\frac{4}{7}$?

Skill 14

A $\frac{10}{7}$ C $\frac{46}{7}$

B $\frac{42}{7}$ D $\frac{64}{7}$

25. Which shows equivalent fractions
for $\frac{5}{6}$ and for $\frac{11}{15}$ using the least
common denominator?

Skill 13

F $\frac{25}{30}, \frac{22}{30}$ H $\frac{5}{30}, \frac{11}{30}$

G $\frac{75}{90}, \frac{66}{90}$ J $\frac{50}{60}, \frac{44}{60}$

Section C: Fractions, Mixed Numbers, and Decimals

Name _____ Date _____ Class _____

SKILL 15: Improper Fractions, Quotients, and Mixed Numbers

A fraction shows division. The numerator is the dividend and the denominator is the divisor.

Example 1

Write $\frac{22}{4}$ as a whole or mixed number.

Divide 22 by 4.

$$4\overline{)22} \quad \begin{array}{r} 5\ R2 \\ \hline 22 \\ -20 \\ \hline 2 \end{array}$$

The 2 in the remainder represents $\frac{2}{4}$, or $\frac{1}{2}$ in simplest form.

$$\frac{22}{4} = 5\frac{2}{4} = 5\frac{1}{2}$$

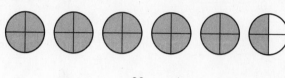

$$\frac{22}{4} = 5\frac{1}{2}$$

Example 2

Write $\frac{18}{3}$ as a whole or mixed number.

Divide 18 by 3. $3\overline{)18} \quad 6$

$$\frac{18}{3} = 6$$

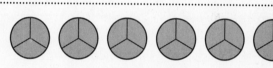

$$\frac{18}{3} = 6$$

Guided Practice

Answer each question.

1. Write $\frac{34}{3}$ as a whole or mixed number.

   a. What is the quotient? _____

   b. What is the remainder? _____

   c. Write the result as a mixed number. _____

2. Write $\frac{62}{9}$ as a whole or mixed number.

   a. What is the quotient? _____

   b. What is the remainder? _____

   c. Write the result as a mixed number. _____

Write each number as a whole or mixed number in simplest form.

3. $\frac{28}{7}$ _____

4. $\frac{4}{3}$ _____

5. $\frac{7}{4}$ _____

Section C: Fractions, Mixed Numbers, and Decimals   Number Theory and Fraction Concepts **33**

SKILL 15: Practice

Write each fraction as a whole or mixed number.
Express fractions in simplest form.

1. $\frac{30}{6}$ _____

2. $\frac{43}{7}$ _____

3. $\frac{14}{7}$ _____

4. $\frac{24}{6}$ _____

5. $\frac{32}{16}$ _____

6. $\frac{48}{8}$ _____

7. $\frac{72}{9}$ _____

8. $\frac{80}{10}$ _____

9. $\frac{16}{5}$ _____

10. $\frac{56}{7}$ _____

11. $\frac{90}{9}$ _____

12. $\frac{68}{11}$ _____

13. $\frac{76}{12}$ _____

14. $\frac{45}{5}$ _____

15. $\frac{38}{19}$ _____

16. $\frac{88}{10}$ _____

17. $\frac{122}{11}$ _____

18. $\frac{96}{6}$ _____

19. $\frac{144}{12}$ _____

20. $\frac{56}{3}$ _____

21. $\frac{39}{9}$ _____

22. $\frac{120}{8}$ _____

23. $\frac{87}{3}$ _____

24. $\frac{67}{4}$ _____

25. $\frac{94}{3}$ _____

26. $\frac{135}{9}$ _____

27. $\frac{91}{7}$ _____

Show each dinosaur measurement as a mixed number.

28. A geranosaurus was $\frac{6}{5}$ m long. _____

29. Each arm of a deinocherius was $\frac{17}{2}$ ft long. _____

30. A hypsilophodon was $\frac{23}{10}$ m long. _____

31. Write $\frac{31}{7}$ as a whole or mixed number.

Skill 15

A 4

C $\frac{4}{7}$

B $3\frac{4}{7}$

D $4\frac{3}{7}$

32. Which shows the mixed number for $\frac{53}{7}$?

Skill 14

F $8\frac{4}{7}$

H $7\frac{5}{7}$

G $7\frac{4}{7}$

J $6\frac{11}{7}$

SKILL 16: Comparing and Ordering Fractions and Mixed Numbers

When ordering mixed numbers, first order using the whole number part. However, sometimes it is necessary to compare or order fractions. One way to do this is to write each fraction with a common denominator.

Example 1

Compare $\frac{3}{4}$ and $\frac{5}{6}$.

To compare the fractions, write them with a common denominator.

Multiples of 4: 4, 8, **12**, 16
Multiples of 6: 6, **12**, 18, 24

The least common denominator of 4 and 6 is 12. Using the LCD, write eqivalent fractions.

$9 < 10$, so $\frac{3}{4} < \frac{5}{6}$.

$$\begin{array}{cc} \frac{3}{4} & \frac{5}{6} \\ \downarrow & \downarrow \\ \rightarrow\frac{9}{12} < \frac{10}{12}\leftarrow \end{array}$$

Since the denominators are the same, compare the numerators.

Example 2

Write the mixed numbers $2\frac{5}{8}$, $2\frac{3}{4}$, and $2\frac{7}{10}$ in order from least to greatest.

Multiples of 8: 8, 16, 24, 32, **40**
Multiples of 4: 4, 8, 12, 16, 20, 24, 28, 32, 36, **40**
Multiples of 10: 10, 20, 30, **40**

The least common denominator for 8, 4, and 10 is 40. Write eqivalent fractions.

$25 < 28 < 30$, so the order of the mixed numbers is $2\frac{5}{8}$, $2\frac{7}{10}$, $2\frac{3}{4}$.

$$\begin{array}{ccc} \frac{5}{8} & \frac{3}{4} & \frac{7}{10} \\ \downarrow & \downarrow & \downarrow \\ \frac{25}{40} & \frac{30}{40} & \frac{28}{40} \end{array}$$

Guided Practice

1. Compare $5\frac{1}{4}$ and $5\frac{1}{6}$.

   a. What is the least common denominator? _____

   b. Write equivalent fractions using the least common denominator. _____

   c. Compare. $5\frac{1}{4} \bigcirc 5\frac{1}{6}$

2. Order $1\frac{5}{6}$, $1\frac{3}{4}$, and $1\frac{3}{5}$ from least to greatest.

   a. Write equivalent fractions using the LCD. _____

   b. Order the mixed numbers. _____

SKILL 16: Practice

Compare using <, >, or =.

1. $\frac{3}{12}$ ◯ $\frac{5}{12}$ 2. $\frac{2}{3}$ ◯ $\frac{1}{2}$ 3. $\frac{5}{8}$ ◯ $\frac{3}{8}$ 4. $\frac{4}{5}$ ◯ $\frac{9}{10}$

5. $\frac{2}{4}$ ◯ $\frac{10}{20}$ 6. $\frac{1}{4}$ ◯ $\frac{4}{13}$ 7. $\frac{5}{7}$ ◯ $\frac{6}{7}$ 8. $\frac{5}{12}$ ◯ $\frac{3}{5}$

9. $4\frac{2}{9}$ ◯ $4\frac{1}{5}$ 10. $4\frac{1}{7}$ ◯ $3\frac{3}{18}$ 11. $6\frac{3}{7}$ ◯ $6\frac{4}{9}$

12. $8\frac{4}{6}$ ◯ $8\frac{12}{16}$ 13. $9\frac{2}{6}$ ◯ $9\frac{4}{12}$ 14. $7\frac{2}{5}$ ◯ $6\frac{5}{11}$

Order from least to greatest.

15. $\frac{3}{4}, \frac{3}{5}, \frac{3}{10}$ 16. $3\frac{4}{5}, 3\frac{3}{4}, 3\frac{5}{6}$ 17. $\frac{7}{10}, \frac{18}{25}, \frac{3}{5}$

_____   _____   _____

18. $5\frac{1}{5}, 5\frac{1}{6}, 4\frac{7}{30}$ 19. $\frac{33}{100}, \frac{3}{10}, \frac{33}{1,000}$ 20. $\frac{49}{56}, \frac{23}{28}, \frac{12}{14}$

_____   _____   _____

Solve.

21. Raoul has $2\frac{1}{3}$ cups of milk. Does he have enough
to prepare a recipe that uses $2\frac{1}{2}$ cups of milk?   _____

22. Fanelli's Hardware stocks wooden dowels in the following widths:
$\frac{3}{16}$ in., $\frac{1}{8}$ in., $\frac{3}{8}$ in., $\frac{1}{4}$ in., $\frac{1}{2}$ in. Write these widths in order from
smallest to largest.

23. Which comparison is correct?

Skill 16

A $\frac{5}{6} < \frac{3}{5}$ C $\frac{2}{5} > \frac{1}{2}$

B $\frac{5}{6} > \frac{7}{9}$ D $\frac{8}{9} < \frac{4}{5}$

24. Write $\frac{53}{12}$ as a mixed number.

Skill 15

F $4\frac{3}{12}$ H $4\frac{4}{12}$

G $5\frac{5}{12}$ J $4\frac{5}{12}$

SKILL 17: Writing Equivalent Fractions and Decimals

You can use a fraction or a decimal to express the same number.

Example 1

Write a fraction for 0.35. Express your answer in simplest form.

number of shaded squares $\longrightarrow \frac{35}{100}$
total number of squares $\longrightarrow$

$\frac{35}{100} = \frac{35 \div 5}{100 \div 5} = \frac{7}{20}$ $0.35 = \frac{35}{100} = \frac{7}{20}$

Example 2

Write a decimal for $\frac{3}{5}$.

You will need to change $\frac{3}{5}$ to an equivalent fraction with 10 or 100 as the denominator.

$\frac{3}{5} = \frac{3 \times 2}{5 \times 2} = \frac{6}{10}$

The picture at the right shows tenths.
6 tenths are shaded.
The decimal for the picture is 0.6. $\frac{3}{5} = \frac{6}{10} = 0.6$

Guided Practice

1. Write a fraction for 0.25 in simplest form.

   a. Write a fraction showing hundredths. _____

   b. Write the fraction in simplest form. _____

   c. 0.25 = _____

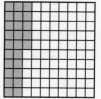

2. Write a decimal for $\frac{11}{20}$.

   a. Write the fraction with a denominator of 100. _____

   b. Write your answer as a decimal. _____

   c. $\frac{11}{20}$ = _____

SKILL 17: Practice

Write a decimal and a fraction in simplest form for each picture.

1.

2.

3.

_____   _____   _____

Write a fraction in simplest form for each decimal.

4. 0.34 _____   **5.** 0.9 _____   **6.** 0.64 _____

7. 0.12 _____   **8.** 0.72 _____   **9.** 0.65 _____

10. 0.4 _____   **11.** 0.27 _____   **12.** 0.32 _____

Write a decimal for each fraction.

13. $\frac{2}{5}$ _____   **14.** $\frac{1}{2}$ _____   **15.** $\frac{9}{20}$ _____

16. $\frac{12}{25}$ _____   **17.** $\frac{3}{4}$ _____   **18.** $\frac{42}{50}$ _____

19. $\frac{11}{20}$ _____   **20.** $\frac{7}{25}$ _____   **21.** $\frac{16}{25}$ _____

Solve.

22. A thumb tack is about 0.85 cm long. Write the length of the thumbtack as a fraction in simplest form.   _____

23. Jason has a drill bit that is $\frac{21}{25}$ cm in diameter. Write the diameter of the drill bit as a decimal.   _____

24. Tonya's caulking gun handle is 0.98 ft long. Write the length of the handle as a fraction in simplest form.   _____

25. What decimal is shown?   *Skill 17*

    A 0.52   C 0.13

    B 0.25   D 1.3

26. Which set of fractions is in order from least to greatest?   *Skill 16*

  F $\frac{2}{3}, \frac{3}{5}, \frac{7}{10}$ H $\frac{2}{5}, \frac{3}{7}, \frac{1}{2}$

  G $\frac{8}{9}, \frac{2}{3}, \frac{1}{6}$ J $\frac{5}{8}, \frac{1}{4}, \frac{3}{7}$

SKILL 18: Dividing to Change a Fraction to a Decimal

To change a fraction to a decimal, divide the numerator by the denominator.

Example 1

Write $\frac{2}{5}$ as a decimal.

To write $\frac{2}{5}$ as a decimal, divide 2 by 5.

The fraction $\frac{2}{5}$ and the decimal 0.4 name the same number.

```
   0.4
5)2.0
 -20
   0
```
← The remainder in the tenths place is zero.

We call 0.4 a **terminating decimal** because it terminates, or ends.

Example 2

Write $\frac{2}{9}$ as a decimal.

To write $\frac{2}{9}$ as a decimal, divide 2 by 9.

The fraction $\frac{2}{9}$ and the decimal 0.222... name the same number.

```
     0.222...
9)2.000
 -18
   20
  -18
   20
  -18
    2
```
← If you keep dividing you always get a nonzero remainder.

The repeating digit can be shown with a bar as $0.\overline{2}$.

We call this type of decimal a **repeating decimal** because a pattern of digits repeats.

Example 3

Write 0.12333... using the bar notation.

Only the digit that repeats is shown with a bar, so 0.12333... is equal to $0.12\overline{3}$.

Guided Practice

1. Rewrite 0.333... using bar notation. _____

2. Rewrite $0.\overline{27}$ using the three dots. _____

Convert each fraction to a decimal by dividing.
Tell if it is terminating or repeating.

3. $\frac{3}{8}$ _____

4. $\frac{7}{9}$ _____

SKILL 18: Practice

Rewrite using bar notation.

1. 0.77777... _____

2. 0.585858... _____

3. 2.656565... _____

4. 7.20222... _____

5. 4.933333... _____

6. 3.001001001... _____

Rewrite using the three dots.

7. $0.\overline{25}$ _____

8. $0.\overline{6}$ _____

9. $2.0\overline{4}$ _____

10. $3.0\overline{27}$ _____

11. $4.7\overline{1}$ _____

12. $9.00\overline{3}$ _____

Write each fraction as a decimal. Tell whether it is terminating or repeating.

13. $\frac{2}{3}$ _____

14. $\frac{7}{10}$ _____

15. $\frac{15}{6}$ _____

16. $\frac{23}{33}$ _____

17. $\frac{1}{8}$ _____

18. $\frac{6}{11}$ _____

19. $\frac{5}{6}$ _____

20. $\frac{21}{40}$ _____

21. $\frac{49}{50}$ _____

22. $\frac{14}{9}$ _____

Solve.

23. A computer word processing program allows users to select a font size of 8 point, 10 point, 12 point, or 16 point.

These sizes are equivalent to $\frac{1}{9}$ in., $\frac{5}{36}$ in., $\frac{1}{6}$ in., and $\frac{2}{9}$ in., respectively. Write each font size as a decimal.

_____

24. Which shows $\frac{4}{9}$ as a decimal?

Skill 18

A 0.4   **C** 0.44

B $0.\overline{4}$ **D** $0.0\overline{4}$

25. What is the simplest form of the fraction shown by the picture?

Skill 17

F $\frac{95}{100}$ **H** $\frac{9}{10}$

G $\frac{19}{20}$ **J** $\frac{1}{20}$

TEST PREP FOR SECTION C

Circle each correct answer.

1. Which comparison is correct?

Skill 16

A $\frac{3}{4} > \frac{5}{6}$ **C** $\frac{8}{9} < \frac{5}{7}$

B $\frac{2}{3} < \frac{5}{8}$ **D** $\frac{3}{7} > \frac{2}{9}$

2. Which is the improper fraction for $7\frac{3}{4}$?

Skill 14

F $\frac{31}{4}$ **H** $\frac{31}{7}$

G $\frac{28}{4}$ **J** $\frac{14}{4}$

3. What is $\frac{45}{3}$ as a whole or mixed number?

Skill 15

A $15\frac{1}{3}$ **C** $4\frac{5}{3}$

B 15 **D** 14

4. Which shows $\frac{2}{3}$ as a decimal?

Skill 18

F $0.\overline{06}$ **H** $0.\overline{6}$

G 0.23 **J** 0.6

5. What fraction is shown?

Skill 17

A 0.24 **C** $\frac{6}{25}$

B 2.4 **D** $\frac{1}{4}$

6. Which shows $\frac{7}{5}$ as a decimal?

Skill 18

F 7.5 **H** 14

G 1.4 **J** 0.75

7. Which shows the improper fraction for $2\frac{5}{6}$?

Skill 14

A $\frac{17}{6}$ **C** $\frac{7}{6}$

B $\frac{12}{6}$ **D** $\frac{16}{6}$

8. Which set of fractions is in order from least to greatest?

Skill 16

F $\frac{3}{4}, \frac{2}{3}, \frac{5}{7}$ **H** $\frac{1}{2}, \frac{7}{8}, \frac{3}{4}$

G $\frac{4}{7}, \frac{1}{2}, \frac{3}{5}$ **J** $\frac{2}{3}, \frac{3}{4}, \frac{5}{6}$

9. What is $\frac{46}{8}$ as a whole or mixed number in simplest form?

Skill 15

A $5\frac{6}{8}$ **C** $6\frac{3}{4}$

B $5\frac{3}{4}$ **D** $4\frac{6}{8}$

10. What decimal is shown?

Skill 17

F 0.19 **H** 1.9

G 0.20 **J** 0.18

11. Which is correct?

Skill 16

A $\frac{2}{3} = \frac{5}{7}$ **C** $\frac{7}{12} = \frac{14}{24}$

B $\frac{5}{6} = \frac{5}{8}$ **D** $\frac{5}{6} = \frac{6}{5}$

12. Which shows the decimal for $\frac{8}{33}$?

Skill 18

F 0.24 **H** $2.\overline{4}$

G 2.4 **J** $0.\overline{24}$

Mixed Review for Section C

Making Cents of Decimals and Fractions

Can you place 4 pennies, 4 nickels, 4 dimes, and 4 quarters in the 4-by-4 square at the right so that no two of the same coin are in the same row, column, or diagonal?

To find one solution, answer each question below. Then match the value of the coin for that exercise with its answer in the 4-by-4 square.

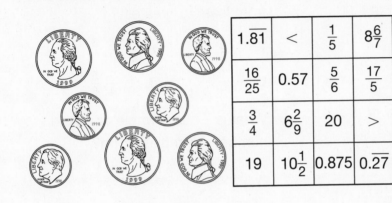

$1.\overline{81}$	$<$	$\frac{1}{5}$	$8\frac{6}{7}$
$\frac{16}{25}$	0.57	$\frac{5}{6}$	$\frac{17}{5}$
$\frac{3}{4}$	$6\frac{2}{9}$	20	$>$
19	$10\frac{1}{2}$	0.875	$0.\overline{27}$

1¢ **1.** Use $<$, $>$, or $=$ to compare.
$4\frac{5}{6}$ ◯ $4\frac{7}{9}$

10¢ **2.** Write the whole number or mixed number for $\frac{57}{3}$. _____

10¢ **3.** Write an improper fraction for $3\frac{2}{5}$. _____

25¢ **4.** Write $\frac{3}{11}$ as a decimal. _____

1¢ **5.** If $\frac{4}{5}$, $\frac{5}{6}$, and $\frac{3}{4}$ were ordered from least to greatest, which would be the greatest? _____

5¢ **6.** What decimal is shown? _____

5¢ **7.** Write $\frac{7}{8}$ as a decimal. _____

1¢ **8.** Write the whole number or mixed number for $\frac{63}{6}$. _____

25¢ **9.** Write a mixed number for $\frac{56}{9}$. _____

10¢ **10.** Write the whole number or mixed number for $\frac{80}{4}$. _____

1¢ **11.** Write $\frac{40}{22}$ as a decimal. _____

25¢ **12.** What fraction, in simplest form, is shown? _____

5¢ **13.** If $\frac{5}{6}$, $\frac{11}{12}$, and $\frac{3}{4}$ were ordered from least to greatest, which would be the least? _____

5¢ **14.** Write a mixed number for $\frac{62}{7}$. _____

10¢ **15.** Use $<$, $>$, or $=$ to compare.
$\frac{4}{5}$ ◯ $\frac{8}{9}$

25¢ **16.** What fraction, in simplest form, is shown?